Old Anniesland to Knigh

with Broomhill, Jordanhill and Scotstou
by Sandra Malcolm

This bungalow in Great Western Road, somewhere beyond Lincoln Avenue, is one of many thousands built by the Glasgow builder John Lawrence. His company folded in 1997. During the air raids of 1941, a number of bombs fell on Great Western Road, but the greatest damage to the area was at Bankhead Primary School on 13 March 1941 at approximately 2100 hours. The school log, written later by the head teacher stated, 'School bombed. Janitor killed. Records destroyed'. Fifteen minutes after the warning sirens sounded, a landmine hit the west wing of the school (the Caldwell Avenue side). Most of the wing was destroyed, as were two houses on the opposite side of the road. The school was also being used as a first aid and Auxiliary Fire Service depot. The memorial plaque at the school lists 39 people who died in the carnage, including the school janitor, his family, men serving in the Auxiliary Fire Service and a number of first aiders. In addition, 80 people were injured. The school was still burning the following day and bits of bodies were being found some six weeks later. White powder discovered in and around the school was tested as there were suspicions that the Germans had resorted to chemical warfare, but after analysis the powder was discovered to be very finely ground pale sandstone from the pillars of the school gates in Caldwell Avenue.

Text © Sandra Malcolm, 2009.
First published in the United Kingdom, 2009,
reprinted 2011, 2013
by Stenlake Publishing Ltd.
01290 551122
www.stenlake.co.uk
ISBN 9781840334746

The publishers regret that they cannot supply
copies of any pictures featured in this book.

Acknowledgements

Many thanks to all those people who gave their
time and energies helping me with this book.
To Kathryn and Rhona, who are my life.

Seen here at Anniesland Cross is one of Glasgow
Corporation's Albion 'Venturers'. In total, the
corporation purchased 268 of these vehicles
between 1935 and 1953. This model had a
highbridge 56-seat body, built by Cowieson of St
Rollox, and was one of fifteen CX 19 models
delivered in 1938. The bus at the rear, No. 267, is
an older AEC Regent. Designed by J.G.
Rackham, these commenced production in 1929.

Further Reading

The sources listed below were used by the author during her research. For more information on them please contact a bookshop or library.

Bryan Cromwell, *Bankhead: The Story of a Primary School at War*, 2001.
Robert Grieves, *Albion album 1899–1999*, 1999.
George Heatley, *St Margaret's Knightswood 1925–1950*, 1950.
Peter Kearney, *The Glasgow Cludgie*, People Publisher, 1985.
Stuart McLean, *History of Jordanhill*, www.wsmclean.com
Sandra Malcolm, *Old Scotstoun & Whiteinch*, Stenlake Publishing, 2003.
Michael Moss, *Range & Vision: The First Hundred Years of Barr & Stroud*,
    Mainstream Publishing, 1987.

Ian G. McM. Stewart, *The Glasgow Tramcar*, Scottish Tramway Museum
    Society, 1994.
Bruce Peter, *100 Years of Glasgow's Amazing Cinemas*, Polygon, 1996.
Williamson, Riches, Higgs, *The Buildings of Scotland – Glasgow*, Penguin, 1990.
Frank Wordsall, *The Glasgow Tenement*, Chambers, 1979.
Claythorn Community Council, *The Claythorn Story*, 1990.
The Glasgow Story, www.theglasgowstory.com
Jordanhill Church 1854–1954, 1954.

Introduction

The areas of Anniesland, Jordanhill, Scotstounhill, Broomhill and Knightswood are all geographically close, yet have their own individual histories. Much of the land was owned latterly by only two families, the Oswalds of Scotstoun and the Smiths of Jordanhill.

The lands from Yoker to Garngad were part of the ancient Kingdom of Strathclyde. King David granted the lands from Whiteinch north-eastwards to the Bishop of Glasgow in the twelfth century. David's grandson, King Malcolm, received help from the Bishop of Glasgow and the Baron of Renfrew when the land was attacked in 1164 by Somerled, Lord of the Isles. As a reward, Malcolm gave the lands of Yoker to Jordanhill to the Baron of Renfrew.

The Oswald family hailed from Caithness. Brothers Richard and Alexander bought the extensive Scotstoun estate in 1748 and it was they who built Scotstoun House. Both men were tobacco merchants, but their business extended to importing wine and sugar from the West Indies, Europe, Virginia and Maryland. Neither brother married and on Richard's death in 1776 the estate passed to his cousin George. His daughter Elizabeth was born at Scotstoun, lived all her life there and died in 1864. Like her predecessors, she carried out many charitable works and gave away plots of land for good causes, such as the Oswald school in Knightswood. When she died, the estate passed to James Gordon Oswald, the grandson of her sister. In turn, it passed to his son, James William Gordon Oswald. Neither man ever lived at Scotstoun, but their interest in the area continued. It was James who built the hall at Anniesland. When he died, one of the conditions of his bequest to his inheritors was that in feuing, selling or letting land, there should be a clause prohibiting the sale or traffic in any 'spirituous or fermented liquor' and this is the reason why so much of the area was 'dry' well into the late twentieth century.

The Smiths of Jordanhill were the last family to own Jordanhill as a complete estate. In 1562, Thomas, the sixth son of Lawrence Crawford, acquired the lands of Jordanhill from Bartholomew Montgomerie, the chaplain of Drumry. Crawford was most likely the builder of the original Jordanhill House which stood on the site of the later one. By 1710, the estate had passed to Lawrence Crawford, who repaired the old house and planted the orchards and gardens. In 1750, Jordanhill was sold to Alexander Houston, a Glasgow merchant. His son, Andrew, built much of the then mansion house in 1782 upon the site of the original house. It is not clear where the name Jordanhill came from, but one theory is that the view from the hill reminded one of the Knights of St John of the Jordan valley and the name Jordanhill was given. Some of the Jordanhill estate extended into Whiteinch, and a number of streets were named after James Parker Smith, Squire of Jordanhill (i.e. James, Parker, Smith, Squire, Jordan and Hill streets).

Balshagray extended from the Clyde to the boundary of Dunbartonshire. Again, it is not clear how the name came into being. An old Gaelic name signifying 'a town or house' is *Bal*, but 'shagray' is not so clear. It is spelt in various ways in the old deeds – it could mean 'the house or town up out of the water' or 'the King's hunting town'. It could also mean 'the priest's town'. The name makes its first appearance in the rent roll of the Bishop of Glasgow, 1509 to 1570. At that time the land was mostly moorland. The Oswald's Scotstoun estate included a large part of Balshagray. The origins of the name Broomhill can only be guessed at. The word 'broom' can be traced to the Scots *brume*. Indeed, broom was particularly plentiful and sought after for use in making brooms, weaving or tying down thatch. And of course, the area is on a hill.

There are various theories about the origins of the name Anniesland. The Glasgow writer Jack House suggested that the name was derived from the Gaelic *annis* meaning 'destitute', or from *anfhann* meaning 'weak and feeble'. To tie in with this idea, there is a theory that the Knights Templar had a hospice in the area. They also rented out plots in this area for annual rents, hence possibly 'Annual-land'. It is also possible that at some point, the land belonged to someone called Annie!

It is generally assumed that the name of Knightswood had an original connection with the Knights of St John of Jerusalem or with the Knights of the Temple. Both orders arose in the early twelfth century. King David I of Scotland and Malcolm IV gave both Orders generous gifts of land. In 1312, the Templars amalgamated with the Hospitalliers, but most records were lost some time during the fourteenth century. However, a deed of Special Retour of Cornelius Crawfurde of Jordanhill, dated 1625, suggests that there was no doubt that the lands of Knightswood had indeed belonged to the Hospitalliers. Much of the land of Knightswood was owned by the Crawfurd family from as early as 1552. In addition, the family had land in Cloberhill (Cowdonhill), Drumry and Jordanhill, as well as land in Ayrshire around Kilbirnie.

Until the early 1830s most of the land in the west of Glasgow was given over to large estates and tenant farms. The development of the area west of the Kelvin truly began on 19 August 1836 when the New Anniesland Turnpike Act received royal assent. Prior to that time, local landowners had owned private turnpike roads, but in 1835 James Gibson (after whom Gibson Street in Hillhead is named) solicited the opinions of more than 180 landowners and occupiers with a view to making Great Western Road a new turnpike road. The bill was steered through Parliament by Sir James Oswald of Scotstoun, MP for Glasgow. One of the main reasons the road is so wide is that the Mowbray brothers (trustees of the Kelvinside Estate) were determined that the road should stretch significantly further than Kelvinbridge (it began at St Georges Cross). The initial plan had been that it would be 60 feet wide to the Kelvin and 40 feet wide thereafter. The Mowbrays insisted that it be 60 feet wide along its entire length and their determination won through. A branch of the Bank of Scotland can be seen here at the corner of Great Western Road and Ancaster Drive. The houses seen in the background, beyond the railway bridge, are rows of identical double villas in red sandstone, designed by Fryars and Penman between 1902 and 1904.

The building on the right is Anniesland Mansions, built between 1907 and 1913, incorporating the columned portico of Anniesland Hall. The hall and mansions were built by James William Gordon Oswald and when he died in the 1930s he left the hall to the Glasgow Evangelistic Association, but they declined the bequest. His widow appointed trustees in December 1941 and church meetings commenced there in 1942. During the 1980s the costs of dealing with the upkeep of the decaying hall were proving hard to meet, and a decision was made to rebuild. When the new building opened in 1990, the main entrance was moved to 796 Crow Road. The new church incorporates some of the oak panelling and doors of the old hall. The Commercial Banking Company was founded in Edinburgh in 1810 and from the outset it issued its own notes. In 1959 it merged with National Bank of Scotland and, in 1970, with the Royal Bank of Scotland. This branch site was later taken over by an office of the Pearl Assurance Company, and more recently the Dunfermline Building Society. On the left, beyond the railway bridge, was the Ascot cinema, the last to be built in Scotland before the Second World War. The auditorium seated 1,900 and was lit with constantly changing coloured light. The opening show was Gracie Fields' *Shipyard Sally* on 6 December 1939. Special precautions had been made in case of air raids. When the siren sounded, the projectionist would display a red slide over the film and when the all clear sounded a green slide was then displayed. The cinema was renamed the Gaumont in 1950 and it became the Odeon in 1964. It closed as a cinema in October 1975 and became for a while the County Bingo Club. The building closed in 1998 and demolition began in 2001. The façade has been kept, and modern flats built behind it.

The cinema at the rear of the tram is the Boulevard, opened in 1928 by William Beresford Inglis. Its entrance faced Knightscliffe Avenue and the side elevation flanked Great Western Road. The building was clad entirely in white stucco and boasted pantile-roofed towers at each corner. Inside were ornate balconies, fancy lighting and a powder-blue ceiling. In 1938, the Singletons bought the Boulevard. According to George Singleton, Inglis had found running cinemas too stressful and wanted to concentrate on hotels. In fact, Inglis opened the famous Beresford Hotel in Sauchiehall Street in the same year as he sold the Boulevard. The Singletons commissioned James McKissack to modernise the cinema and the seating capacity was increased to almost 1,500. It reopened as the Vogue in 1939. It closed in 1959 and was demolished in 1960. Glasgow Standard tramcar No. 638 came into service in 1904. Refurbished in February 1930, it was scrapped in October 1956. To the extreme left of the picture, a bus can be seen turning into Knightswood garage. It was opened in 1932 and, at the time, it was the largest garage in Europe. Much of the design had been modelled on Berlin's municipal garage. It took nine months to build at a cost of £60,000. The garage ceased to operate in 2004 and has since been demolished; around 250 new homes have been built on the site. The block of tenements on the right was built between 1937 and 1942 as part of the Great Western Road housing scheme. Higher quality tenements such as these were recommended by the 1935 Highton report, 'Working class housing on the continent', and 433 houses had been built on each side of Great Western Road by 1942.

When Elizabeth Oswald of Scotstoun died in 1864, her estate passed to her sister's grandson, James Gordon, who adopted the Oswald name. In the family tradition, he was very concerned with the spiritual welfare of his tenants, although he never lived at Scotstoun himself. He appointed a Christian factor for the estate, a Mr Crosbie from Ireland who took up his post in 1878. Oswald built the first Anniesland Hall which opened in 1868. In 1881 a big evangelical campaign was organised for the Anniesland district and a gospel tent was pitched in the grounds of what is now the High School of Glasgow (to the right of the photograph). Oswald withdrew the use of the hall from the Free Church and appointed one of the evangelists from the tent campaign as the first pastor of Anniesland Hall. Oswald's son built the newer Anniesland Hall and Anniesland Mansions. When the new hall opened, the old hall became a reading room and library for the district, books provided by Oswald. The hall closed when Bearsden Road was built in the 1920s. This photograph dates from 1936; in 1901, Anniesland Cross was still very rural, where cows could be seen grazing – there were no street lights between the Cross and Clydebank. The toll house for the turnpike road stood roughly on the site of the toilets just to the left of the picture. These in turn were replaced by the high flats known as Anniesland Court, Scotland's tallest listed building, built between 1966 and 1968.

Crow Road is referred to in old documents and maps as 'The Craw Road' which is taken from the Gaelic *Crodh*, meaning cattle. It is therefore likely that Crow Road was a drove road for Highlanders bringing their cattle to the city. The cottages towards the right of the photograph have been largely unaltered externally since they were built. Continuing a pre-existing development known as Fern Cottages, they were built in 1885 to house workers on the Scotstoun estate. These dwellings were superior to many workers' cottages of the period as the Oswald family was keen to build high quality housing at affordable rents for their estate workers, and similar properties were built in Elm Street, Lime Street and Park Street in Whiteinch. By 1966 Fern Cottages had been sold to their occupants. The approach roads to the Clyde Tunnel have meant that this is now a very busy thoroughfare, much changed from the rural area that the cottages stood in originally.

Ancaster Drive takes its name from the Earl of Ancaster who owned 6,407 acres of rough farmland around Loch Katrine. Ancaster sued Glasgow Corporation for £500 because during the construction of the Glasgow Water Supply he lost fifteen acres of land. The street was first listed in 1897. A variety of shops have occupied the areas on either side of the drive: a wool shop, Paterson the butcher, Rogerson the newsagent, the Tea Cosy, and many more. Ancaster Drive itself boasted a branch of Cochrane's, the well-known grocery chain. Most of the shop fronts have since been altered to some extent, although the Dunfermline Building Society further along at 1627 Great Western Road appears to be largely intact. At the top of the building on the right there are drying greens on the flat top roof. The room provided for the domestic help within the flats was tiny in contrast to the generous proportions of all the other rooms. Glasgow Corporation had several proposals put before it for the building of public conveniences at Anniesland. In 1912, the corporation agreed to the construction of a built urinal with six stalls and roofed over, the site being Ancaster Lane. The ground belonged to the North British Railway Company.

The cottages on the right of this view of Landsdowne Avenue are the earlier part of the development known as Fern Cottages. At the time, they were considered very modern as they had a water supply from Loch Katrine. The supply was inaugurated in October 1859. To begin with it was available in the street from a locked box. A key cost five shillings per year. Until that time, water came from a local spring which usually dried up in the summer. Close inspection of the brickwork shows crosses over the doorways and for a short time the cottages were known as Chapel Row. The railway line seen in the background was opened in 1874 and must have made the cottages very dirty from the soot of the trains. The cottages had wash houses with coal-fired boilers for heating water, along with sinks and scrubbing boards. More cottages in Fern Lane (the Crow Road cottages seen on page 8) were added in 1885. Around 1931, several streets and roads had to be renamed because there were already streets of the same name within Glasgow and Lansdowne Avenue became Sackville Avenue.

Anniesland Station was opened by the North British Railway on 20 October 1874 and was known as Great Western Road Station. The station was on the North British Railway's Stobcross Branch, opened in the 1870s as a freight-only route to the Stobcross (later Queen's) Dock, but linked into the city centre in 1886 by the opening of the Glasgow City & District Railway. The station became part of the London and North Eastern Railway during the Grouping of 1923 and then passed on to the Scottish Region of British Railways on nationalisation in 1948. It was renamed Anniesland in 1931. One of the difficulties with Great Western Road was the width of the railway bridge at Anniesland Cross. A new bowstring lattice girder bridge was installed in 1930 when the road was widened. Both station buildings seen here are of standard North British Railway timber and brick construction. The timber edging to the awnings was cut back when the line was electrified in 1960 and the buildings were demolished in 1969 and replaced by modern structures. The other railway in the area was the Cowdenhill Branch line, also part of the North British Railway. It encircled much of Temple, coming from Jordanhill Brickworks, passing Garscube Brick & Tile Works and Robinson & Son Temple Sawmills.

To the right of the photograph is the site of Temple Gas Works, established in 1871 by the Partick, Hillhead & Maryhill Gas Company to supply those areas outside the Glasgow City boundary at the time. In 1891 the works were bought by Glasgow Corporation, who closed it down, supplying gas from its nearby Dawsholm Gas Works instead. The gas holders here are the ones built by the corporation in 1893 and 1900 when they converted the works into a storage depot. The holders have a combined storage capacity of 254,867 cubic metres. Dawsholm Works, which supplied the gas stored in these holders, stopped producing coal gas in 1964, though it later produced gas by reforming naphtha, a product of petroleum refining. The holders now store natural gas. In the left background is Dawsholm Park. Glasgow Corporation purchased the area that now forms the park from Sir Archibald Campbell of Succoth in 1922. The wooded area of the park was part of Sir Archibald's Garscube Estate and was known as the Belvidere plantation. An area of blaes bings (waste oil-shale mounds) to the east of the woodland was gifted to the corporation free of charge by Sir Archibald due to the cost of carrying out remedial works and this was levelled by the corporation to form a recreation area.

Howth Terrace in Temple was constructed in the late 1890s. Until the 1880s, most of Temple was farmland. In the early 1890s, a farm stood where Temple Gardens stands now. The farmer's name was Fulton, after whom Fulton Street is named. Ralston Terrace and Stephen Terrace were built around the same time as Howth Terrace. The valuation rolls of 1913/14 show that all the houses in Howth Terrace were occupied by tenants and there was a shop at No. 2, probably a dairy, run by Mrs Janet Alexander. Most of the tenants were skilled men, with jobs such as engineers, sawmillers, signalmen and instrument makers. Many of these men would have been employed locally in businesses such as Temple Sawmills (founded in 1874), Dawsholm Paper Mills (founded in 1783) and later on Netherton Works (founded in 1914). The present-day Howth Terrace is further north of the original one shown here.

The founder of Methodism, John Wesley, first visited Scotland in 1751. In all he made 22 visits to Scotland between then and 1790. Most of his journeys were to the east coast, Glasgow and the south-west. In May 1784 he preached in Elgin where he blessed the son of his hosts, Thomas Sellar and his wife Jane. The boy he blessed was Patrick Sellar, the Factor of the Sutherland Estates in the nineteenth century and the principal agent of the Highland Clearances. The church in Temple is noted in the 1906 Dumbarton Register of Sasines when Sir Archibald Spencer Lindsay Campbell of Succoth feued 353/1000 of an acre of ground at the corner of Howth Terrace and Sutcliffe Street to 'the Superintendent Preacher of the people known as Methodists'. In 1932 the three principal stands of Methodism, the Wesleyans, United Methodists and Primitive Methodists united to form the modern Methodist Church of Great Britain. The red sandstone building in Bearsden Road is now the main place of worship, with the ground at the rear being the original site for the temporary building seen above. The Church celebrated its centenary in 2003.

Linden Place is situated just behind Temple Police Station on Bearsden Road. The police station opened in 1905 and came into Glasgow in October 1912 when the city boundaries were extended to take in Partick Burgh and Govan Burgh. Although relatively rural at the beginning of the twentieth century, Temple was opened up to industrialisation by the arrival of William Baird & Son, structural engineers, around 1890. They built a new engineering shop in 1913 at a cost of £2,500 along with a seven-bay office block. An earlier arrival in the area was Robinson Dunn & Company (Temple Saw Mills), whose timber yards, founded in 1874, occupied a large area beside the Forth & Clyde Canal, the canal being used as a timber pond. Between 1931 and 32, Bearsden Road was driven through the mills. The children in the picture would have attended Temple Primary School, which opened when the old school at Netherton was no longer viable. The school was built on Spencer Street and designed by the architect Henry Higgins. It opened in 1901 for the New Kilpatrick School Board and was expected to accommodate 1,040 pupils after an extension was added in 1906. The school closed in the summer of 2007 and pupils were relocated to Knightswood Primary.

The church on the right of the picture was Temple Parish Church, in existence from 1892 until 1984. Temple was part of the parish of New Kilpatrick. In 1873 a mission began and the site for a church was donated by Lady Campbell of Garscube. £3,740 had to be raised to build the church and in 1892 the first service was held there. There were 120 members when the church first opened, but over the next twelve years the congregation grew to 455. Much of this was because of the influx of workers into the area. The first minister, the Rev. James Carswell BD served there for 44 years. In 1908 Mrs Smith of Jordanhill gifted a new manse in Helensburgh Drive to replace the one in Ancaster Drive. After the First World War ended, a memorial plaque was unveiled by James Parker Smith of Jordanhill Estate, who was MP for the area and had been a member of the church since it opened. The name of his own son was on the memorial – Lieutenant Parker Smith – alongside 26 other men from the parish. During the Second World War, the church was used by Barr & Stroud for training the Home Guard, and the Post Office used it to deal with the large amount of mail over the Christmas periods. After the war, in common with many churches, initially there was a large increase in membership, but gradually numbers fell and the last service was held on 24 June 1984. The congregation voted in favour of amalgamating with Anniesland Cross Parish Church. The building was sold, converted briefly to an indoor skateboard park and later demolished.

The church on the left, across from Barr & Stroud, had its roots in Maryhill. A number of people moved into the area from there in search of work and their minister, William Duncan of Maryhill United Presbyterian Church, encouraged them to petition for a preaching station to be opened in Anniesland. By 1899 a hall had been built and in 1905, John Stephen of Linthouse laid a memorial stone in the new church, which opened in 1906. At that time the church had 214 members. In 1929, the United Free Church joined with the Church of Scotland and by 1956 the congregation boasted a membership of over 900. After a parish visitation in 1961 membership rose to 1,004. In 1965, the new housing development at Anniesland Cross was announced and the minister, the Rev. Dr Harry C. Thomson was directly involved in negotiations with the council. The church received £1,250 for a piece of ground the corporation took over, and used this as an opportunity to fundraise for a new hall. When the Rev. Ian MacDougall, the minister of Temple Parish, died in 1982, Glasgow Presbytery intimated a union of the two churches and the service of union took place on 27 June 1984. At that time, Anniesland had a congregation of 669 and Temple 153. The amalgamation led to the church being designated Temple-Anniesland Parish Church.

Archibald Barr was born in 1855 in Glenfield, near Paisley and was educated at Paisley Grammar School. He began an apprenticeship at a local firm of boilermakers and engineers, and also took a degree in engineering at Glasgow University. Barr completed his degree in 1877 (having completed his apprenticeship in 1876) and immediately was appointed to the post of 'Young Assistant' to James Thomson, Regius Professor of Civil Engineering and Mechanics (and brother of Lord Kelvin). Barr left Glasgow University in 1884 to become Professor of Engineering at the Yorkshire College of Science in Leeds. In 1885, he met William Stroud. Stroud was born in Bristol in 1860 and went to Clifton College, a local grammar school where he won a scholarship to study at University College, Bristol. In 1879 he won another scholarship to study at Owen's College in Manchester and he graduated with a first in Chemistry in 1882. He left Manchester to pursue further studies at Oxford University after winning another scholarship to study there. In 1884 he graduated with a double first in Mathematics and Natural Sciences. After a spell of study in Germany, he returned to London to sit examinations for his doctorate. Thereafter, he took up the post of Cavendish Chair of Physics at the Yorkshire College of Science in Leeds.

Barr and Stroud met for the first time in 1885. In 1887 they started work together devising a lantern-slide camera, which after being patented two years later, became standard equipment in most British colleges and universities. In 1888, they replied to a War Office advert inviting engineers to submit a design for a new rangefinder for military use. Barr and Stroud constructed their instrument. Stroud drew up the specifications for the lens and prisms and sent them to Thomas Cooke and Sons of York, while Barr obtained the mechanical parts they required from James White & Co. in Glasgow. All the components were brought back to Leeds and the two men tested their instruments in a lane near the college. Although the War Office was interested in the design, both men decided to use cheaper materials in the trials. Unfortunately the rays of the sun heated and distorted the mirrors and therefore the War Office rejected their invention. Despite the

set backs, the men continued to develop their invention, but found it increasingly difficult because of the costs involved. Barr left Leeds for Glasgow in 1889 when he was appointed as Regius Professor of Civil Engineering at the university. This meant that he and Stroud had to continue much of their work by post. In 1892, they submitted another instrument for new trials of rangefinders by the Admiralty. This time their instrument was accepted and the Admiralty ordered five. At this time, Barr and Stroud had no premises as such, and after ordering parts from various manufacturers, Dr Barr and a workman named Sinclair Reid assembled the instruments in Dr Barr's home, 'Royston', in Dowanhill. After receiving orders from foreign navies, Barr and Stroud realised that they could no longer make their instruments at home, and decided to set up a business, Barr & Stroud Patents, and began by renting property in 250 Byres Road in July 1895. An increasing demand for rangefinders meant that the company had to expand, and more premises were rented at 230 Byres Road in 1897. By 1899, the men realised that demand was increasing again and they expanded their empire to include 44 Ashton Lane, behind Byres Road. This gave them additional space and allowed them to take on more employees. There was a machine shop on the ground floor, a fitting shop on the first floor and a testing area in the attic. A platform was also built on the roof to allow the range of the instruments to be tested. By 1902, the company employed at least 65 men.

Becoming aware that the business was reliant on only one product, both men began looking at ways to diversify. In 1899 they began to sell small vacuum pumps, Becker clocks, and patented a variety of other inventions. Sales of all products amounted to £20,889 in 1903 and a profit of £5,630 after tax was recorded. Harold Jackson became a junior partner and the three men decided to open a new factory to allow them to expand even further. They chose a site at Anniesland, part of Scotstoun Estate, beside Robert MacLehose & Company's new printing works. The ground cost £648 in July 1902 and work began in 1903.

The office block was designed by Alexander Paterson, a Glasgow architect. It faced a private road, which the firm named Caxton Street. The office complex contained a workers' canteen, a kitchen and strong room on the ground floor. On the first floor there was the general office, cloakrooms, a waiting room, audit room and Dr Barr's private room. The adjusting shop for the rangefinders was on the top floor. Behind the office building was a workshop built by Sir William Arrol & Company and designed by A.C. Auden, their engineer. It was a single-storey brick building with a glass roof. Inside was the machine shop, grinding department, a general store, a work-in-progress store, a tool shop, paint shop and an optical grinding room. Even when the factory was nearly completed, Barr and Stroud realised that it was still too small and another building was erected on the west side of the machine shop, to house fitting and assembly shops. Another one was built to the north, separated from the rest of the works by a lane, to reduce the potential danger of fire. It contained a foundry, pattern shop, smithy, paint shop and packing case store. In 1906 further extensions were added, two storeys being added to the west bay of the machine shop.

At the outbreak of the First World War, the Admiralty and War Office requisitioned all rangefinders in stock at Anniesland, and before the end of 1914 they had placed orders for 3,283 new instruments. In order to cope with this demand, nightshifts were introduced and the works extended. Around a hundred employees were called up and, in 1916, 20 women started with the company; by 1917 there were 312. After the war orders from the military decreased and in 1919 the firm began the manufacture of cinematographs, binoculars and 'Impactor' golf machines. Valves for motorcycle engines were also produced. While doing this, the company was still producing rangefinders, many for the Japanese, and in the 1920s they were the sole suppliers of submarine periscopes to the Royal Navy. By the late 1920s they were experimenting with the manufacture of aerial survey instruments. In 1931 Dr Barr died, and Dr Stroud was in semi-retirement (he died in 1938) but the business went from strength to strength. By 1937 the factories were extended and a new three-storey building was built at the north-eastern end of the original site. Two storeys were added to the building on Crow Road and Strathcona Street, and the West works was extended to the west and north. By 1939 the factory employed 2,000 workers, and by 1944 that number had trebled. Lord Haw Haw broadcast from Nazi Germany that German bombers would destroy 'that little toyshop in Anniesland' and Luftwaffe photographs were later discovered which had Barr & Stroud marked as targets. The glass roof was painted over with camouflage colours and air raid shelters were built beneath the West Works. In 1945, when the House of Commons was being rebuilt after bomb damage, the architect asked Barr & Stroud to provide a periscope 'to enable the ventilation control engineer to see how many Members and Strangers are in the chamber at any moment, and where they are grouped, so that the ventilation can be adjusted accordingly'. This was installed in 1950, and the firm was also involved in the replacement of the camera obscura in Edinburgh. By the mid 1950s, Barr & Stroud moved towards electronics as a way of keeping their place in the market, although optical components were still a large part of their business. In 1977, the firm became a subsidiary of Pilkington Bros Ltd. Because of the volume of defence work in the 1980s, Barr & Stroud had to find more factory space at Anniesland and the works of Robert MacLehose & Company next door, which they had purchased and leased out and then used as a store, became an area used to develop new manufacturing techniques such as visual, infrared and laser technologies. In 1994, the company moved to new premises at Linthouse, and the Safeway Supermarket chain built a new superstore on the site.

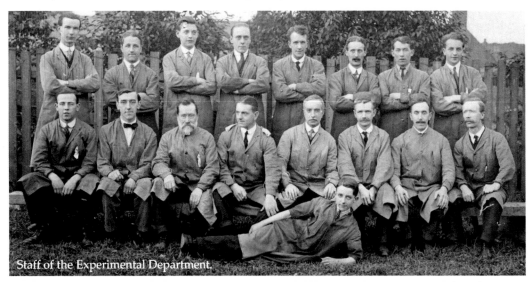

Staff of the Experimental Department.

Barr & Stroud supplied over 16,000 FT17 and FT27 field rangefinders, seen here, between 1913 and 1918. In addition, the French armies had over 30,000 of these, along with earlier models. The firm was keen to provide a working environment that was both clean and safe. The glass roofs allowed for natural light into the building and the floors were cleaned every lunchtime. They provided their employees with khaki overalls at cost price, sinks were fitted with plenty of soap and towels laid on, and spitting on the floors was forbidden and spittoons provided. Unlike most other firms in Glasgow, the men did not start work until 8 a.m. and the standard working week was 50 hours. The men also worked under a bonus scheme (the Rowan scheme), introduced in 1901 and continuing until 1932. A year after the factory opened, Barr & Stroud had 252 employees.

During the First World War, unions were concerned that the employment of women was used as a means of depressing wage rates, but at Barr & Stroud the management promised not to use women in the machine shop (seen here) and to pay them a wage equivalent to that of newly recruited male workers. The power for the belt driven machinery was provided by a gas engine until a new electricity generating substation was opened by Glasgow Corporation at Anniesland in 1915. The doors at the end led to a private lane, across which was the pattern shop, paint shop and inflammable goods store.

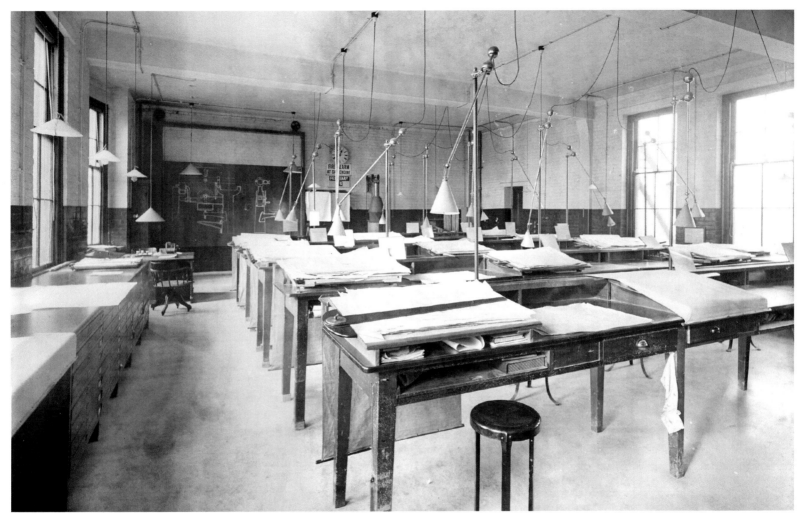

The Drawing Office. It was Barr & Stroud's policy to train apprentices to the highest standards. They were expected to complete five years of training and were only allowed to move on to more difficult jobs once they had perfected the previous ones. Dr Barr encouraged apprentices to attend evening classes and they could earn bonuses depending on their attendance and how they fared in examinations. Those who did well were also encouraged to continue their studies at Glasgow University.

Much of the area of Scotstounhill was owned by the Oswald family of Scotstoun Estate. Richard and Alexander Oswald bought the estate in 1748 from a Glasgow merchant William Crawfurd. They built Scotstoun House on the south side of Dumbarton Road, just south of Ardsloy Place. When Richard died in 1776, the estate passed to their cousin George, who in turn passed it to his daughter Elizabeth. In 1825 she added a new front to the house, designed by David Hamilton. She was very generous to local communities and had a great interest in education. Contemporary writers describe her as a 'genuine Scotchwoman, of a type, we fear, extinct: despising the modern love of luxury and excitement, looking on the young generation as a race of spoiled children . . . [she is] . . . fine-mannered, hospitable, methodical, busy almost to the last in works of religion and charity'. When she died in 1864, she bequeathed £50 to the poor of each of the parishes of Renfrew and Govan. On her death the estate passed to James Gordon Oswald, the grandson of her sister, but he spent much of his time travelling abroad or at his estate in Aigas, Beauly. His son followed the same tradition, although still took a keen interest in the area. Much of the estate was sold off for housing in the later part of the nineteenth century. Anniesland Road runs all the way from Dumbarton Road to Anniesland Cross. The houses above (Sherwood and Ainslie) were built around 1891 and are beside the entrance to Scotstounhill Station.

In June 1966 an application for a 'shopping and housing development' was lodged with Glasgow Corporation and most of the villas shown in this 1906 postcard of Anniesland Road were demolished to make way for the shopping centre. Only the villas in the distance remain. In 1895 an ordnance survey map shows Anniesland Road with the villas above the last residential dwellings on the western boundary of Scotstounhill. Anniesland Road meets the top of Queen Victoria Drive, originally Oswald Drive and for a while known as Victoria Drive, named after the owners of Scotstoun Estate. Until the late nineteenth century, most of the west lands of the estate were rural, with farms dotted about.

The area to the right of this photograph would have formed part of Scotstoun Mains farm which covered a large part of Scotstoun Estate and can clearly be seen on maps dated 1864. Some of the villas to the left are in Queen Victoria Gate, and further to the right are those in Southbrae Drive, Jordanhill. 'South Brae' appears on John Ainslie's map of 1796, but most of the houses along its length were built between 1900 and 1920.

At the start of the twentieth century, Scotstounhill was effectively only a small cluster of houses near Scotstounhill Station. The villas on the left were constructed by the McIntosh Company of Glasgow after James Gordon Oswald had feued parts of the Scotstoun Estate specifically for that purpose. It was around this time that Scotstoun Primary School moved to its present site in Duncan Avenue and the houses between Lennox Avenue and Verona Avenue were built by the Scotstoun Estate Building Company. The area to the right of the photograph would have formed part of Scotstoun Mains farm. In the inventory made after Miss Oswald's death, the proprietor of the farm was listed as George Richmond. His arrears for rent at that time was £355/15/3*d*. In the mid 1930s, the land was used as an annexe for Victoria Drive Higher Grade Public School, opened in 1909. The school was situated at the corner of Queen Victoria Drive and Larchfield Avenue. It closed in the late 1990s.

This *c*.1900 picture shows the top end of Queen Victoria Drive before Lincoln Avenue was formed. On the left are a row of four Edwardian bungalows (Nos. 227–233) with unusual dormers on wide hipped roofs. Title deeds to 223 Queen Victoria Drive reveal that this villa was created on Oswald land feued from James Gordon Oswald in favour of John Edwards, builder with the McIntosh Company and dated 13 August 1886. The villa took just over eighteen months to build and it was then sold in 1888 to John Dugald Parker, a Glasgow tea merchant, for £560. A number of the villas in Queen Victoria Drive built by the McIntosh Company were named after works of the Canadian author, Lucy Maud Montgomery: Kilmeny, Ingleside and Avonlea. It is probably coincidence, but in 1488 Scotstoun Estate passed from royal Stuart hands to the Montgomeries of Eglinton who owned the land for 200 years. Vancouver Road in Scotstoun was formerly known as Montgomerie Road before Scotstoun became part of Glasgow with the passing of the 1926 Boundaries Act.

Talbot Terrace, Scotstounhill, pictured *c*.1910. In the distance can be seen the shop attached to Scotstounhill railway station on the other side of Anniesland Road. Camouflaging a railway cutting carrying the North British Railway line running from the city to Balloch and Helensburgh are the mature trees on the right. Wynne Talbot Crosbie was manager of the Scotstoun Estate Building Company, which built most of the houses on Scotstoun Estate. Educated in Glasgow High School he was the third son of Lindsay Talbot Crosbie, the factor of Scotstoun Estate for 23 years. In and around the Scotstounhill area were a number of farms. On Southbrae Drive, to the east, was Windyedge Farm, belonging to the Stirling Family. The farm existed well into the twentieth century – Mr Stirling made a claim against Glasgow Corporation in 1925 for damage to his fields when Anniesland Road was being widened. Muttonhole Farm (sometimes known as Scotstounhill Farm) can be seen on maps of 1795. It was farmed by the Coubrough family and covered most of modern day Scotstounhill. One of the last owners of the farm was Thomas Coubrough who died in 1923. High-rise flats and post-war housing now occupy the site.

At the corner of Anniesland Road, further south of Lincoln Avenue stood Muttonhole Cottages. These buildings were entirely separate from Muttonhole Farm. In fact, they were on the land belonging to Windyedge farm. To the right of the cottages in this photograph from around 1905 can be seen Muttonhole School. To the left of them is the redbrick schoolmaster's house. In 1790, George Oswald of Scotstoun spent five guineas towards the purchase of this house. There is little information about this school, but it was probably run by the parish. By 1919 the cottages had been demolished, although the school building still stood at that time.

Scotstounhill railway station opened in 1887, as part of the Glasgow, Yoker and Clydebank Railway (later taken over by the North British Railway Company). Built as a commuter station, it served the needs of an ever-increasing population. In the same year as the station opened, Bartholomew's Gazetteer reported that 'Scotstown is noted as a village with railway station … within Renfrew Parish, population is 757.' By 1914, the area had been completely transformed by large-scale building of residences. Although the present-day entrance is off Anniesland Road, there used to be another way in from the Queen Victoria Drive side. In keeping with common practice at the time, the station had a shop attached to it. In 1910, the stationmaster was William Gray and the junior shopkeeper was Miss Bissett. The buildings were more elaborate than other stations of their kind and were possibly built to compliment the large villas surrounding it.

In the Mitchell Library an old manuscript contains an entry explaining the meaning of 'Balshagrie Avenue'. It states that *Balshagrie* (the old spelling) means 'the windy town' and continues that, 'The Avenue is formed on the lands of that name; the quaint single-storey mansion stands on the west side with the date 1641 over the door. These lands with Hyndland, Skaterigg and Scotstoun have been in the possession of the Oswald family since the middle of the eighteenth century. They had in the olden time been church lands within the Bishopric of Glasgow and the superior has accordingly bestowed upon the thoroughfares names of an ecclesiastic nature such as Abbey Drive, Bishops Road and Dean Road.' Other sources suggest *Balshagray* is the Gaelic for 'the town of the decayed or withered flock' or a corruption of different Gaelic words meaning 'the town of the hunting of the king'. *Balshagray* also contains the Gaelic *baile* ('farm', 'estate'), probably qualified by *seagalach* ('rye-producing'). There were two farms at Balshagray: Low Balshagray and High Balshagray. Most of Low Balshagray disappeared when Victoria Park was laid out in the 1880s. Much of high Balshagray covered what is now south Jordanhill. Rents for the farms were paid to Miss Oswald of Scotstoun Estate. The farmhouse belonging to High Balshagray was demolished in 1928 as the demand for land for housing grew.

The area of Broomhill was laid out around 1870 on the western edges of Partick. Marlborough Avenue led down to Balshagray Avenue, which overlooked Victoria Park. Originally, Balshagray Avenue was the main road to Balshagray Mansion, built in 1641 by John Stewart, the last member of that family to be connected with the estate. William Crawfurd of Jordanhill repaired the house and it was he who created the avenue. Balshagray Estate lay to the west of Partick and extended from Great Western Road to the River Clyde. Part of the Great See of Glasgow, it was first mentioned in 1509.

The villas and tenements of Woodcroft Avenue, Naseby Avenue and Marlborough Avenue were completed between 1888 and 1910. Designed by Whyte and Kennedy, the houses round the oval in Marlborough Avenue were built in 1902 on the north side and 1907 on the south side. Nos. 1–24 are houses designed by William Baillie in the Glasgow Style, with Art Nouveau leaded stained glass and tapering chimneys. These were built around 1903, while most of the area to the north of Victoria Park was not laid out until around 1910. In 1913, the land at the bottom end of Marlborough was owned by Mr Espie, dairyman. By 1913 many of the houses in Marlborough were tenanted by professionals – engineers, admiralty officers, tea merchants, teachers and accountants.

Behind the tenements of Broomhill Mansions is Randolph Road where Broomhill Parish Church is situated. Founded in 1899, Broomhill Church was originally Broomhill United Free Church. The red sandstone church was opened in 1902 and the hall in 1899. Both the hall and church were designed by Stewart & Paterson, and the latter has stained glass by Guthrie & Wells. Also in Randolph Road is Jordanhill Bowling Club, founded in 1899 with one rink and a 'bowl house', and still in existence today. Further up Crow Road, on the opposite side is Broomhill Lawn Tennis and Squash Club. Founded around 1920, Tom and John Inglis bought a field on Crow Road belonging to Scotstoun Estate. After four blaes courts were laid out, a wooden clubhouse was opened in 1922. One of the club's more famous members was A.E. Pickard who lived in Mitre Road nearby. Pickard was a millionaire renowned for his eccentric ideas and showmanship. He made his money through buying up properties and it was said that the only landlord who had more property than he did was Glasgow Corporation. He began his property empire by purchasing Fell's Waxworks in the Trongate. He then added an American Museum before purchasing the Britannia Music Hall which was above his waxworks. He changed the name to the Panopticon and Stan Laurel made one of his first stage appearances there. Pickard was also the first man to be booked for a parking offence when he parked his car in the middle of Platform 8 of Central Station when he thought he was going to be late for his train. He paid the £1 fine with a £100 note.

A police signal box at the corner of Crow Road and Clarence Drive; first introduced in Glasgow in 1891, and designed by Charles Eggar, police boxes were intended to provide 'communication of visible signals and establishing electrical and telephonic connection between central, town and district (police) stations'. The boxes were manufactured by MacFarlane & Company at its Saracen Foundry. Inside the box were gaslight fittings, electromagnetic coils, levers, pulleys and telecommunications equipment. The box could be used by a police officer to contact his station by telephone, or the station could contact the police officer by lighting the gas lamp on the top of the box to indicate that the officer should contact the station. Initially the police force purchased fourteen boxes at a cost of approx £500. Such was their success, 56 boxes were in use around the city by 1914. Beyond the tenements can be seen the construction works which became Marlborough Mansions and beyond that is the present site of part of Broomhill Primary School. The school opened in 1955 in Randolph Road and had a roll of approximately 285 pupils. By contrast, at the same time, Whiteinch Primary had 838 pupils and Scotstoun Primary had 931. By 1960, Broomhill's roll had increased to 350. The annexe on Crow Road is used for pupils from primaries one to four.

Crow Road Station was on the lower part of Crow Road. The station opened on 10 October 1896 as part of the Lanarkshire and Dumbarton line running from Dumbarton along the north bank of the Clyde to Partick. The station had an island platform and was situated under Clarence Drive. The next station on the line was Kelvinside Station. The station was closed on 6 November 1960 as part of the Beeching cuts and although it was demolished in 1970, the platform can still be seen. Further down from the station towards Dumbarton Road, and on the opposite side, was the Tivoli cinema, designed by Benny & Blain. It was opened in 1929 with an auditorium built for 1,900. It had rows so wide that seated customers did not have to stand to let people through. In addition, it boasted a Christie Organ to try to encourage people to leave the Rosevale in Partick. In 1932 it was bought over by Gaumont and after the Second World War Gaumont was taken over by Rank. The building changed its name to the Classic, but closed in 1972.

This house on the corner of Victoria Park Gardens South and Balshagray Avenue was demolished to make way for the Clyde Tunnel developments in the 1960s. Before the tunnel, Balshagray Avenue was a long leafy avenue with a number of large mansions on it. Oswald Villa was built for the minister of Whiteinch Free Church and Northfield Villa was the manse for Partick Free Church. The church tower belongs to what was originally Whiteinch Congregational Church, opened in 1907 and designed by J.J. Burnett. The congregational originally used Whiteinch Lesser Burgh Hall for their meetings for the ten years prior to the building of the church. When the church closed, the building was adapted into flats.

Broomhill Drive runs from Broomhill Cross down to Dumbarton Road. At the top of the drive, to the extreme left of the picture is Balshagray Victoria Park Church. The church was dedicated on 11 September 1909 and halls were added in 1911. Up until the early 1990s the church was simply called Balshagray, but 'Victoria Park' was added to the name when the congregations of Balshagray and Victoria Park were united. Victoria Park Church had been in Balshagray Avenue until it was demolished in the 1960s to make way for the Clydeside Expressway. A modern church was built to replace it at the bottom of Broomhill Drive, but it too was demolished and houses were built on the site. The tenements in Broomhill Drive were part of a development begun in 1871 by the Victoria Park Feuing Company Ltd. The later tenements at the top of the drive, Inverclyde Gardens, were added in 1902. Towards the bottom of the drive, on the left-hand side is a SSHA development, built on the hill between 1963 and '69. Originally there had been six large villas on the hill. The five eighteen-storey tower blocks were built to house those displaced by the construction of the Clyde Tunnel. Opposite them, a further three eight-storey blocks were built around the same time.

Like Broomhill Drive, the tenements in Broomhill Avenue were built by the Partick Feuing Company Ltd, although these were built later, in 1885. At the bottom of the drive was Balshagray Public School, built by Govan Parish School Board and opened in 1904. In 1948 it had a roll of between 651 and 850 pupils, but in 1949 Hamilton Crescent Junior Secondary annexed part of the building while primary school education continued in some of the classrooms. Hamilton Crescent School closed in 1972 and the building was taken over by Anniesland College. The hill at the right of the photograph is where the five eighteen-storey tower blocks were built in the 1960s. One of the mansions that was demolished for these can just be seen at the top of the hill at the end of the avenue.

Jordanhill House was built between 1782 and 1784 by Andrew Houston, who had bought the estate in 1700 from the Crawfurd family. The estate covered 285 acres and was in the Parish of Renfrew. It is believed that the land was originally owned by the Poor Knights of Christ and the Temple of Solomon at Drumry, but in 1338 the land was passed to the Livingstone family. In 1800 Andrew Houston sold the estate for £14,000 to Archibald Smith, who made additions to the house at a further cost of £4,000. When the land was advertised, it was described as 'delightfully situated about four miles westward of Glasgow' and the grounds consisted of 227 Scots acres and contained trees 'which may be thinned to advantage'. Archibald Smith had made his fortune trading in tobacco first with Virginia and North Carolina, then subsequently with the West Indies. When he died in 1821, he was succeeded by his son James who was greatly interested in science and theology. He had many friends who were Arctic explorers and Cape James, Cape Mary (his wife's name) and Jordanhill Island are all named after him. His mother Isobel Smith lived until she was 101, and she was a contemporary of Elizabeth Oswald who died in her 97th year. It was James Smith who was instrumental in having the protective glass roof building placed over the fossils in Victoria Park. On James's death, his son Archibald inherited, but only six years later he too died and his widow Susan Parker Smith inherited the estate. By this time the estate was in financial difficulties and she feued off huge parts of the estate for housing. She preferred to live in Putney and never actually lived at Jordanhill. She died in 1913, leaving the properties to her son James Parker Smith. He became MP for Partick and was Joseph Chamberlain's Parliamentary Private Secretary. In 1913 the house and the remainder of the estate was sold to provide accommodation for a Teacher Training College.

The first railway in Jordanhill was a goods line to Whiteinch on the Hyndland to Anniesland line. The Whiteinch Railway Company had opened this line in 1874 and in 1891 the North British Railway Company bought the line and introduced passenger services in 1897. In 1882, the Glasgow, Yoker and Clydebank Railway opened a line from the Stobcross Branch to serve the Clydebank shipyards. It was this line that included a new bridge over Crow Road. Shortly afterwards, Singer built its sewing machine factory in Clydebank and there was a huge increase on passenger demand between Glasgow and Clydebank. In 1893 the line became twin track and was extended to join the Helensburgh line at Dalmuir. Originally the station had a booking office, waiting rooms and ladies' and gentlemen's lavatories. These wooden buildings were replaced in 1969. The 1913 Ordnance Survey map shows a station built to serve the Glasgow Agricultural Society Showgrounds. It was situated behind what are now the Lawrence houses in Southbrae Drive. However, there is no sign of the station by 1932. Although not brought into service until 1930, the bridge over the line at Westbrae Drive was built in 1928, and spanned the passenger line as well as the goods line.

A map of 1793 shows Crow Road as a well-established road, leading from Dumbarton Road to Anniesland Toll and then further up to the canal. It opened on 28 July 1790 and one of the first expenses Archibald Smith had was for gravelling the 'footpath from Dumbarton Road to Anniesland Toll by Balshagrie'. On the east side of Crow Road were the lands of Gartnavel, much of which was farmland. The houses on the right were built between 1909 and 1911 (Nos. 554–620 Crow Road). During the same period the houses and shops at Nos. 542–550 Crow Road were also constructed. Further up Crow Road, towards Anniesland Cross, in the area of Ancaster and Willoughby Drives were allotments which were removed in 1947 to make way for prefabs. Around 1900 there was a cycle racing track on the site. To the south stood the Great Western Steam Laundry, Nos. 459–463 Crow Road. Built in 1885, this was the first mechanised laundry in Glasgow. It was intended that most of its business would come from wealthy customers in the west end suburbs. As washing machines became cheaper and more readily available, the business declined in the 1950s and the company was taken over by Initial Services, finally closing in the 1970s. The laundry building was demolished and a car showroom is now on the site.

Some of the housing developments in south Jordanhill can be seen here at the rear of the Victoria Park bowling greens. In a map of 1859 south Jordanhill is mainly arable land with only two buildings. By 1895 a number of large villas south of Abbey Drive had appeared and there was one house on York Avenue (now Eastcote Avenue). There was a rifle range and 'flagstaff' in the middle of a field where St Thomas Aquinas Secondary School now stands. Before the original school was built in 1953, the land was owned by John Lawrence and he intended to extend his housing developments there. However, a compulsory purchase order was put on it by Glasgow Corporation because a large site was necessary for a new Roman Catholic school. In 1924 (after this photograph was taken) the Balshagray Building Company in Buchanan Street advertised houses being built in a development around Westland Drive, Essex Drive and Mitre Road. Cost ranged between £811 and £928 and a bond of 80% could be had from the corporation. Any houses unsold after three months would be taken over by the corporation. After the development was completed, twelve houses at the western end remained unsold and the corporation took them over as council houses.

The church in the centre of the picture is Jordanhill Parish Church. Founded in 1854 in a school set up by Miss Oswald of Scotstoun, the church was originally called 'Hillhead Free Church' and was an offshoot of Renfrew Free Church. When the church building was first opened, it was situated on School Brae just off Knightswood Road on land granted by Miss Oswald. Over time, the name was confused with the area of Hillhead nearer Glasgow and the church briefly changed its name to 'West Hillhead'. By 1873, the name had gone back to 'Hillhead' and it remained as this until 1888, when it was agreed to change the name to 'Jordanhill' after receiving permission from Mr Smith of Jordanhill to do so. At the beginning of the twentieth century, the congregation started to fundraise for a new church building, and after procuring the site in Woodend Drive from Mrs Smith of Jordanhill, the new church opened in 1905. The ground had previously had been the garden of Woodend Cottage, the home of Mr Gilchrist of Messrs Goldie and Gilchrist of Woodend Brickfield. Munro Road is named after the Rev. G.D.R. Munro, minister of Hillhead Free Church from 1874 till 1902. Concerned with the welfare of some of his parishioners, he had advised some of the miners in the area to build their own homes, hence Munro Place. On a site near Munro Road was the Compass Observatory. One of Lord Kelvin's interests was terrestrial magnetism and he started making (and calibrating) very accurate compasses. His firm 'Kelvin and James White' was making compasses in the early 1900s and in order to produce accurate compasses, he needed a testing centre away from the factory. Jordanhill was very rural and an ideal site for such a venture.

Woodend Drive was named after Woodend Cottage which stood on the site of the present Jordanhill Church. It was once known as the Back Road as estate workers used it to get from Crow Road to the stables and gardens of Jordanhill House. The local brickworks were also called Woodend. The church at the right of the photograph is All Saints Episcopal Church. The existence of this church began when Jane Charlotte Smith, who lived in Jordanhill House with her parents, visited miners' cottages in the area and decided to start a school for the inhabitants. She began lessons in Jordanhill House itself, and then in a barn where Episcopal services were also held. Her father gave her a plot of land near Crow Road and on All Saints Day 1861 she opened a chapel school, with a roll of 120 children. However, after visiting the sick in the area, she contracted typhus and died in 1864, aged 35. As membership of the church school grew, the congregation decided to raise funds for a permanent building. The school itself had closed in 1892 and in 1904, on All Saint's Day, the new church was dedicated. The memorial stone had been laid by Archibald Parker Smith on behalf of his great aunt, Sabina Paisley, Jane Smith's sister. Later a rectory was added and St David's, a mission church in Whiteinch, opened at the top of Lennox Avenue. In the first fifteen years of the church's existence, the congregational roll grew from 270 to over 600. The original rectory was demolished in the 1990s to make way for a new housing development, but a new rectory was later built beside the church.

Jordanhill College of Education has its origins in the work of David Stow who sought to educate children to raise them from poverty. He wanted to develop 'the whole man' and believed that such an important task as teaching should not be left to an untrained person. His first school opened in 1828 in the Drygate and attracted 'student-observers' who came to find out how subjects were being taught. In 1832, the school moved to larger premises in Saltmarket, but by 1834 it had become clear that 'the real cause of defects in the system of parochial instruction . . . is the want of professional training'. Funds were sought and Dundas Vale Seminary opened in 1837. After the Disruption of 1843 the Dundas Vale buildings became the property of the Church of Scotland and Stow opened his new Free Kirk Seminary, now known as Stow College. The school had eleven staff, 93 students and 700 children. Generally the teacher training course lasted one year and David Stow sought to teach his students the art of communication between teacher and pupil. Initially, he placed his students with the youngest children to force them to think of their material in terms of a child's ability to understand. Schools like Stow's were founded in Aberdeen and Edinburgh and by the beginning of the twentieth century, it was obvious there was a need for a national approach to teacher training. In 1920 the National Committee for the Training of Teachers was formed and the Glasgow Provincial Training College opened at Jordanhill in November 1922. From 1920 to 1959 the college was conducted by the Glasgow Provincial Committee for the Training of Teachers. In 1958 the college was renamed Jordanhill College of Education. The original Jordanhill House was demolished in 1961 and the Crawfurd Building was erected on the site. The sundial in the forecourt was originally in the garden of the house. In 1981 Hamilton College was absorbed in Jordanhill and in 1992 Jordanhill became an Associate Institution of Strathclyde University. On 1 April 1993 it merged with the university and formed their Faculty of Education.

Jordanhill School is set off Chamberlain Road and was designed by Honeyman, Keppie & Mackintosh in 1913 and completed in 1920 by Keppie and Henderson. It was formerly run by Jordanhill College of Education as its demonstration school and was previously known as Jordanhill College School. Pupils who attended had to have their books, jotters and of course uniform purchased by their parents. Classes in the school were small, although by 1921 there were nineteen pupils in the secondary department. Pupils would have been used to rows of students sitting in their classes watching demonstration lessons and then taking their turn at teaching the class. By 1922 ten college staff were involved in part-time instruction in the school. In 1926 tennis courts were formed and in that same year, pupils were presented for the first time in the Leaving Certificate Examination. In 1936, the school fees were three guineas per term for the primary and five guineas per term for the secondary. At the beginning of the Second World War, pupils were taught in a variety of buildings in the college such as Woodend pavilion, Rothley pavilion and Barclay Curie's pavilion when the military authorities requisitioned the school grounds. The school has a unique status. It is now funded by a direct grant from the Scottish Executive and is neither a local authority school nor a private or independent school.

Woodend Bowling and Tennis Club in its current site on Chamberlain Road was formed in 1909 as an offshoot of Jordanhill Bowling Club. The Smiths of Jordanhill agreed to feu land and the cost of forming the two greens, four tennis courts and a pavilion was estimated at around £1,500. Six months later, on 5 June 1909, the opening ceremony took place. Before long the original clubhouse was found to be unstable and a new clubhouse was opened at a cost of £2,900, although it has subsequently been demolished when some of the land was sold off for a new housing development in the area. A new pavilion has since been erected. Other tennis and bowling clubs existed in the area. In 1925 Castlebank Laundry (which stood on the north side of Anniesland Road, east of the row of cottages known as Compass Cottages) formed the bowling green and tennis courts for its employees and called it the Rossley Bowling Club. In 1945 the site was purchased by Yarrow and Company Ltd for their employees and a second bowling green was laid out. It became the Yarrow Recreation Club. Barclay Curle Recreation Ground (now Burlington Gate housing development) also had two bowling greens and a pavilion. Anniesland Bowling and Tennis Club at 101 Helensburgh Drive was founded in 1931 by City Bakeries for use by their staff. Drysdales Pumps became the new owners in the 1960s, and then in the mid 70s the premises were acquired by Weirs of Cathcart. Because they already had a staff bowling club in Cathcart they called this club 'Weirs of Yoker'. When Weirs decided to sell in 1977 the members bought the club and called it Anniesland Bowling and Tennis Club once again.

Until the late 1880s, much of Knightswood was farming land. The church in this photograph, St Margaret's, was built on a field that had been Knightswood Farm. In 1886, the land was described as 'arable land of excellent quality, capable of growing all kinds of green and white crops'. In the same document, reference was made to the expansion of Glasgow and noted that building sites 'may soon be taken up'. However, it was not until 1920 and 1921 that Glasgow Corporation made their first purchases of land to begin the Knightswood Housing Scheme. In 1923 the Presbytery of Dumbarton of the Church of Scotland proposed to build a new church to serve the community of Knightswood. On 1 October 1925 the Knightswood Housing Scheme was officially opened by Prime Minister Stanley Baldwin when he and his wife opened two new houses at the corner of Cowdenhill Road, later renamed Baldwin Avenue. The same year the church hall was completed after donations were received from all other churches in the parish. In its first year, the congregation had 127 members; by 1927, there were 312 persons on the roll, and a Sunday school of 450 children. The church building itself was designed by Sir Robert Lorimer and after considerable fundraising, the building opened in 1932. By this time the congregation had risen to nearly 1,000, with 752 children attending Sunday school. The church had originally been known as 'Knightswood Church', but after the union between the Church of Scotland and the United Free Church in 1929, the current name was adopted.

A total of 6,714 houses were built on both sides of Great Western Road from 1923. Four new shopping centres, eight churches and six schools were also provided. The houses were all no more than two storeys and included semi-detached, terraced houses and cottage flats. The land was bought from the Summerlee Iron Company (see next page) and building work was carried out over three phases – 1923–1926, 1926–1931 and 1931–1940s. In 1929 Glasgow Corporation acquired 148 acres of land for Knightswood Park. In addition to the two bowling greens and four tennis courts, the park included a golf course, pitch and putt course, boating pond, running track and cricket pitch. The council had banned the opening of pubs in Knightswood (as the Oswalds had previously done on their land in Scotstoun and Whiteinch) and the park was an attempt to change the social habits of the residents away from alcohol to more healthy activities.

It is not clear when mining came to Knightswood, but it is mentioned in the *Statistical Account of Scotland* of 1793. In that year, Knightswood Colliery employed 60 men and boys and 20 horses, but the *Account* also states that the coal was nearly exhausted. A map of 1795 shows an engine house just south of Cloberhill House and the old 'Red Town', probably the original colliers' cottages. In 1841 Wilson's & Company took out a 99-year lease and they developed the coal and ironstone workings in deeper strata. In this connection, they built the first part of Knightswood Rows (seen here). By the second part of the nineteenth century, the two other rows had been built, a total of 115 houses. The population grew from 319 in 1861 to 790 in 1881. The ironstone was calcined, then taken to the ironworks at Coatbridge. Between Cloberhill and Knightswood Rows were nine different pit shafts. The Summerlee Iron Company, who built the rest of the rows, had a shop at the end where people were expected to spend their earnings. Other traders were not allowed and barriers were erected to prevent vans and carts entering the rows. The company also owned a public house, known locally as 'The Rat-pit'. By 1896 the pits had closed and many of the miners transferred to Blackhill Colliery near Maryhill. Many of the blaes heaps were then used for brickmaking, including over six million bricks for Glasgow Corporation from 1920. The Rows had no water or toilets in the houses and water was obtained from communal taps. The outside toilets were back to back with the ash pits. The women did their daily washing outside in huge shared vessels containing boiling water. By the 1930s the rows were considered too unsanitary for occupation and were condemned. They were demolished in the late 1930s. The large building in the right background is Knightswood Hospital.

When Glasgow Corporation built the new estate at Knightswood, many of the street names reflected the link with mediaeval times. Some of the names were taken from Scott's 'Tales of the Crusaders', for example Ivanhoe Road, Talisman Road, Templar Avenue, Rotherwood Avenue, Athelstane Road and Rowena Avenue. Other names reflect the period – Crusader Avenue, Warden Road and Kestrel Road. Dunwan Avenue, seen here, is named after Dunwan Hill near Eaglesham, which is thought to have had a hill fort or a nobleman's house at the top. Before the estate was built, Knightswood Hospital opened in 1877 as a Joint Infectious Diseases hospital. The land was bought from Mr Oswald of Scotstoun on very favourable terms. Spanning fourteen acres, it had a central house accommodating 20 patients and two pavilions, each housing 20 patients. Costing £15,000 to build, it served the burghs of Partick, Maryhill and Hillhead. In 1887 a new pavilion was added as an isolation block for smallpox cases. When Glasgow Corporation took over in 1912, the number of beds had risen to 90, but by 1938 this number had increased to 200 and there were now nine pavilions. It changed from a fever hospital to a general one in 1963. It closed in 2000 when most of its specialities were returned to the Western Infirmary in Partick. The site, opposite the present Knightswood Secondary School, has since been used for housing.

Baldric Road, Knightswood. The area was previously served by Partick Fire Station but as the area grew it was decided to open a new station at 373 Anniesland Road, on the corner of Ryvra Road, to serve Knightswood, Yoker, Whiteinch and Drumchapel. When opened in 1958, it had accommodation for two appliances and two other vehicles and was built at a cost of £55,000. Eighteen firemen were stationed there initially, although by 2000 this number had risen to 28. As Knightswood developed, the corporation gave consideration to library facilities in the area. In 1933 an experimental book distribution centre opened in Temple School, but this proved to be unsuitable because it was so far away from the area. A temporary library was opened in 1934 after Knightswood Temporary School opened near Knightswood Cross. After the war, accommodation in the school was tight, so the library moved to the east wing of the community centre, which had been designed as a health clinic. It was not until 1969 that construction work began on a specially designed library on Dunterlie Avenue, as part of the community centre for the area, at a cost of £75,000. The library opened on 10 February 1971.

Alderman Road is one of the main arteries running from east to west through Knightswood. This block of shops was rebuilt after a major fire in the early 2000s. During the Second World War, many bombs fell on Knightswood as the Luftwaffe aimed for Clydebank and the shipyards. On Thursday, 13 March 1941, 250 German bombers headed for Clydebank and bombs landed in Trinley Road, Cowdenhill Avenue, Friarscourt Avenue, Baldwin Avenue, Ferenze Crescent and Fulwood Avenue. North of Great Western Road, 44 houses were wrecked. A bomb fell on a pavement outside 77/79 Boreland Drive and the house at No. 81 collapsed. All eight members of the family trapped inside were rescued. On 7 May four bombs fell on Knightswood, roughly parallel to Kestrel Road, and one demolished houses in Baldric Road. A few days later, four bombs were dropped immediately behind Knightswood Bus Garage. The first two did not explode and local residents had to be evacuated to Temple School while they were made safe. It seems that the police and the air raid wardens in the area did not get on. On this occasion the police were accused of being more interested in the Head Warden's car and its lack of blacked-out headlamps than they were in the unexploded bombs. Allegations were also made that the police had been seen drinking tea in the engineer's room at Knightswood Hospital when they were meant to be searching the grounds for more unexploded bombs. The matter was serious enough for the Chief Constable Percy Sillitoe to order an enquiry into the matter, although the allegations proved groundless.